Knowsburg 1a 2788

9/2011

5 311 787

Homes

Kimberley Jane Pryor

Smart Apple Media
P.O. Box 3263
Mankato, MN, 56002

First published in 2010 by
MACMILLAN EDUCATION AUSTRALIA PTY LTD
15–19 Claremont St, South Yarra, Australia 3141

Visit our web site at www.macmillan.com.au or go directly to www.macmillanlibrary.com.au

Associated companies and representatives throughout the world.

Copyright © Kimberley Jane Pryor 2010

Library of Congress Cataloging-in-Publication Data

Pryor, Kimberley Jane.
    Homes / by Kimberley Jane Pryor.
        p. cm. — (Animal lives)
    Includes index.
    Summary: "Gives information on types of places animals live in and highlights different animals, both large and small from land to sea"—Provided by publisher.
    ISBN 978-1-59920-404-8 (library binding)
    1. Animals—Habitations—Juvenile literature. I. Title.
    QL756.P79 2012
591.56'4—dc22
                            2010046006

Publisher: Carmel Heron
Managing Editor: Vanessa Lanaway
Editor: Paige Amor and Georgina Garner
Proofreader: Tim Clarke
Designer: Ben Galpin
Page layout: Ben Galpin
Photo researcher: Lesya Bryndzia (management: Debbie Gallagher)
Illustrator: Ben Spiby
Production Controller: Vanessa Johnson

Manufactured in the United States of America by Corporate Graphics
North Mankato, Minnesota
April 2011

Acknowledgements
The author and the publisher are grateful to the following for permission to reproduce copyright material:

Front cover photograph of leopard gecko, courtesy of Shutterstock/Cathy Keifer.

Michel Gunther/Biosphoto/Auscape, **8**; Gary Bell/Corbis, **15**; Anthony Bannister/Gallo Images/Corbis, **25**; Jason Edwards/National Geographic/Getty Images, **16**; iStockphoto.com/Andy Gehrig, **14**; iStockphoto.com/Kolby Henrie, **9**; iStockphoto.com/Frank Leung, **4**; iStockphoto.com/Susan McManus, **26**; iStockphoto.com/Paul Morton, **22**; iStockphoto.com/Steve Ralston, **28**; NOAA/Monterey Bay Aquarium Research Institute, **19**; Photolibrary/Age Fotostock/Bartomeu Borrell, **23**; Photolibrary/Animals Animals/Paul Freed, **12**; Photolibrary/Michael Giannechini, **30**; Photolibrary/Oxford Scientific (OSF)/Mary Plage, **10**; Photolibrary/Superstock/Barry Mansell, **13**; Photolibrary/Maria Zorn, **24**; Shutterstock/Mari Anuhea, **27**; Shutterstock/Marianne Bones, **29**; Shutterstock/DMSU, **5**; Shutterstock/Cathy Keifer, **17**; Shutterstock/NatalieJean, **18**; Shutterstock/Mark R, **20**; Shutterstock/teekaygee, **11**; Shutterstock/Chris Turner, **21**.

The author would also like to acknowledge the following sources for information used in this book:
Magnetic termite: Theodore Evans and Claire Manson, CSIRO and Steve Vogel, the Australian Museum.

While every care has been taken to trace and acknowledge copyright, the publisher tenders their apologies for any accidental infringement where copyright has proved untraceable. Where the attempt has been unsuccessful, the publisher welcomes information that would redress the situation.

For Nick, Thomas and Ashley

Contents

Glossary Words

When a word is printed in **bold**, you can look up its meaning in the glossary on page 31.

Animal Lives

Animals face many challenges in their lives. From the moment they are old enough to look after themselves, they have to work hard to survive. They must search for food. They need to escape from hungry **predators**. They have to find or make safe homes so they can shelter from the weather and hide from danger.

When they become adults, animals must attract mates so they can have young. Some animals travel to faraway **breeding** grounds to have their young. After they hatch or are born, many young need to be protected and cared for until they, too, are old enough to survive on their own.

To face the challenge of sheltering from the weather, this elf owl has made a home in a hole in a tree, made by a woodpecker.

All animals need homes in which to live. A home provides shelter from the weather and protection from predators. An animal can live in the same home all year if it is near food, water, and other animals of the same type. An animal moves from its home if it needs to find food, water, or a mate. Some animals make a special home, such as a nest, in which to raise their young.

Different Types of Homes

Different animals live in different types of homes. Some animals live in plants, or under logs or rocks. Some animals build homes. They find housing materials, such as leaves or sticks, or make their own materials, such as beeswax or silk.

Storks make huge nests out of sticks.

Village Weaver

Village weavers are birds that live in **colonies** in hot, dry parts of Africa. The males weave globe-shaped nests out of grasses and other plants.

Several male village weavers build their nests in a tree. Each male chooses a branch from which his nest will hang. He then lands beside fresh green grass, snips off a long, thin strip, and flies back to the branch he has chosen.

When the nest is finished, the male village weaver hangs upside down under it and flaps his wings to attract a female. A female chooses a male that has a fresh, green nest.

The male village weaver makes a thin, **vertical** ring out of strips of grass. He uses several different stitches and knots to weave the strips of grass together.

The male village weaver adds more strips of grass to the vertical ring. He makes a rounded nesting chamber and an entrance.

Chimpanzee

A chimpanzee lives high up in the trees. It climbs or swings from tree to tree to find fruits, leaves, and insects to eat.

Chimpanzees build fresh nests out of branches and leaves to sleep in each night. Mother chimpanzees share their nests with their young. Other chimpanzees build and sleep in their own nests. Chimpanzees sleep about 12 hours each night.

FACT FILE

Type of Animal: mammal

Head and Body Length: 3 feet (90 cm)

Habitat: rain forests, woodlands, and grasslands

Distribution: Africa

Housing Materials: branches and leaves

Did You Know?

A chimpanzee usually builds its nest 32.8 to 65.6 feet (10 to 20 m) above the ground.

During the day, a chimpanzee will sometimes rest in a bowl-shaped nest in a tree.

Young raccoons climb around the entrance to their den when they are about eight weeks old.

Did You Know?

A raccoon can leave its den by walking down the tree headfirst!

Raccoon

A raccoon usually makes its home, called a den, in a hollow tree. It uses its den for resting, sleeping in the winter, and raising young.

Raccoons usually live alone, but they sometimes share their dens with other racoons. They usually rest in their dens during the day and hunt for food at night. In very cold weather, they sleep in their dens for several weeks. Young raccoons live with their mother in a den lined with leaves.

 FACT FILE

Type of Animal: mammal

Head and Body Length: 1.6–2.1 feet (50–65 cm)

Habitat: woodlands and marshlands

Distribution: Europe, Asia, and North and South America

Housing Materials: leaves

Plants and Flowers ·············

Honduran white bats hang upside down under a heliconia leaf during the day.

Did You Know?

When the sun shines through a heliconia leaf, it makes a Honduran white bat's fur appear green. This helps to **camouflage** the bat.

FACT FILE

Type of Animal: mammal

Head and Body Length: 1.4–2 inches (3.5–5 cm)

Habitat: rainforests

Distribution: Central America and the Caribbean

Housing Materials: leaves

Honduran White Bat

A Honduran white bat makes its home out of a heliconia leaf. The leaf protects the bat from the sun, rain, and predators.

Honduran white bats choose large leaves that are about 6.6 feet (2 m) above the ground. They cut through veins on the leaves with their teeth so each leaf folds into a tent shape. A single leaf can shelter between 1 and 12 bats.

Flower Spider

A flower spider is very hard to see because it lives on a flower that matches the color of its body. It uses camouflage so it can surprise **prey** and hide from predators.

A flower spider waits for an insect, such as a bee or a butterfly, to land on its flower. It then rushes forward and grabs the insect with its long front legs. The spider bites the insect on the head and sucks out its insides.

 FACT FILE

Type of Animal: invertebrate

Length: 0.12–0.47 inches (3–12 mm)

Habitat: forests, woodlands, and gardens

Distribution: every continent except Antarctica

Housing Materials: none

Did You Know?

A flower spider often stays on a flower until the petals become soft and limp. It does not share the flower unless it is ready to mate.

A flower spider is the same color as the flower on which it lives.

Mexican Free-tailed Bat

A Mexican free-tailed bat usually lives in a colony in a cave. A cave is a safe place for it to rest during the day.

Mexican free-tailed bats hang from the ceiling of the cave during the day. In this position, they are out of reach of most predators, and they are also warm and dry. A single cave can be home to 20 million bats!

FACT FILE

Type of Animal: mammal

Head and Body Length:
3.5 inches (9 cm)

Habitat: caves, bridges, and buildings

Distribution: North, Central, and South America

Housing Materials: none

Did You Know?

Female Mexican free-tailed bats fly as far as 994 miles (1,600 km) to special nursery caves every summer. There, they raise their young.

About 4 million female Mexican free-tailed bats give birth to their young in this cave in Texas.

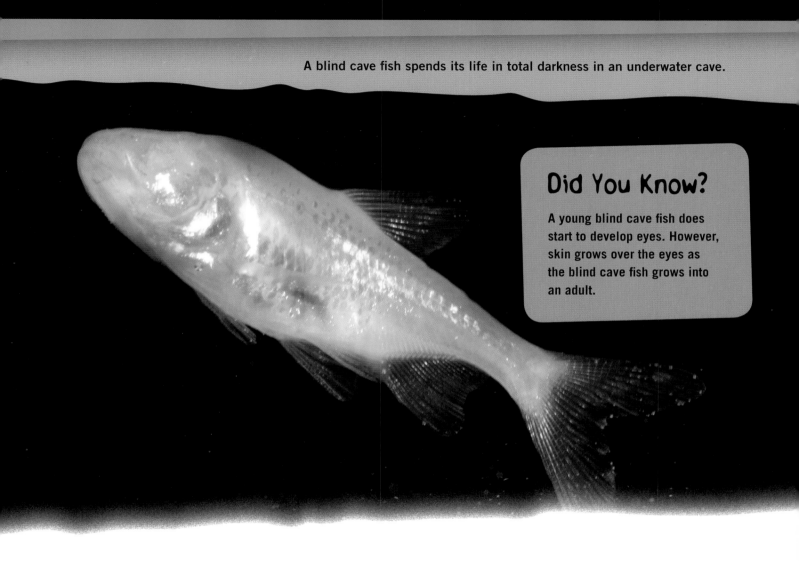

A blind cave fish spends its life in total darkness in an underwater cave.

Did You Know?

A young blind cave fish does start to develop eyes. However, skin grows over the eyes as the blind cave fish grows into an adult.

Blind Cave Fish

A blind cave fish lives in an underwater cave in a stream or river. This is because there are fewer predators in a cave than near the water's surface.

Blind cave fish have no eyes and no coloring because they do not need them in the dark. They can sense changes in water pressure, so they hardly ever bump into anything. They can also sense food, so they are able to find enough to eat without seeing.

 FACT FILE

Type of Animal: fish

Length: 4.7 inches (12 cm)

Habitat: streams and rivers

Distribution: North and Central America

Housing Materials: none

13

Burrows ....

A mound of soil around the burrow entrance helps protect black-tailed prairie dogs from predators and floods.

Did You Know?

The largest prairie dog town ever found covered 25,000 square miles (65,000 sq km). It was home to about 400 million black-tailed prairie dogs!

 FACT FILE

Type of Animal: mammal

Head and Body Length: 11.8–15 inches (30–38 cm)

Habitat: grasslands

Distribution: North America

Housing Materials: grass

Black-tailed Prairie Dog

A black-tailed prairie dog lives in a colony in a huge burrow system called a prairie dog town. The prairie dog town provides places to hide from predators.

Black-tailed prairie dogs dig burrows and line them with grass. The burrows have rooms for sleeping, storing food, and raising young. Black-tailed prairie dogs share their burrows with family members, but a **pregnant** or **nursing** female does not share her nursery burrow.

Spotted Garden Eel

A spotted garden eel lives in a colony in a burrow in the ocean floor. It hides in the burrow if it senses danger.

Spotted garden eels dig burrows on sandy slopes that are exposed to **currents**. They never fully leave their burrows. Instead, they stretch up to feed on tiny animals that are carried by currents. When mating, two eels lean out of their burrows and twist their upper bodies together.

FACT FILE

Type of Animal: fish

Length: 15.7 inches (40 cm)

Habitat: sandy slopes near coral reefs

Distribution: Indian and Pacific oceans

Housing Materials: none

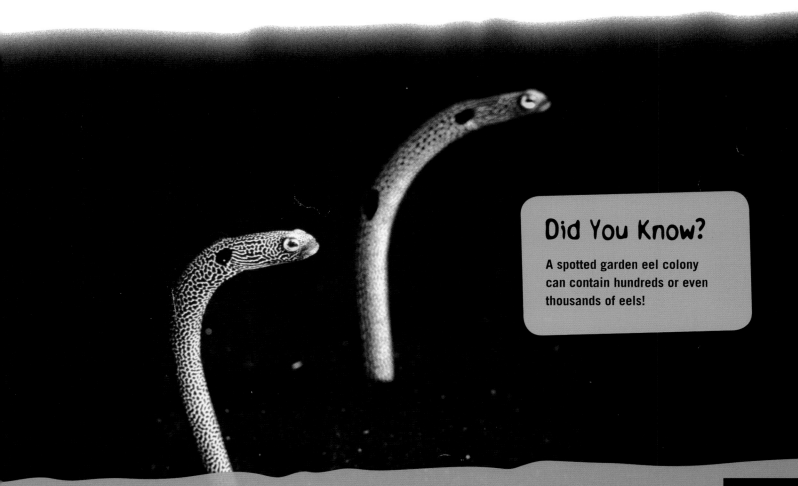

Did You Know?

A spotted garden eel colony can contain hundreds or even thousands of eels!

Spotted garden eels live in burrows that are near each other.

FACT FILE

Type of Animal: mammal

Head and Body Length: 2.4–3.5 inches (6–9 cm)

Habitat: woodlands, shrublands, grasslands, and farmlands

Distribution: Australia

Housing Materials: grasses and other plants

Fat-tailed Dunnart

A fat-tailed dunnart usually lives under a log to avoid very hot and very cold days. It uses grasses and other plants to make a nest under the log.

A fat-tailed dunnart sleeps in its nest during the day. It sleeps alone in the summer to keep cool, but it often cuddles up to other dunnarts in the fall and winter to stay warm.

Did You Know?

A fat-tailed dunnart rests in its nest in the winter or when food is scarce. It stores fat in its tail to help it survive.

16   Fat-tailed dunnarts sometimes shelter in hollow logs.

A leopard gecko shelters under rocks to protect itself from very hot and very cold weather.

Did You Know?

A leopard gecko usually rests during the coldest part of the winter. This is how it copes with the drop in temperature and the lack of food.

Leopard Gecko

A leopard gecko usually lives under a pile of rocks. The rocks protect it from the extreme temperatures found in dry grasslands, sandy deserts, and stony deserts.

Leopard geckos live in habitats that have baking hot days in the summer and bitterly cold days in the winter. They hide under rocks during the day and come out in the evening to hunt for insects to eat.

FACT FILE

Type of Animal: reptile

Length: 5.9–9.8 inches (15–25 cm)

Habitat: grasslands and deserts

Distribution: Asia

Housing Materials: none

Sometimes two moray eels share a hole in a coral reef.

Did You Know?

A moray eel can swim backward. This allows it to quickly enter a hole or crevice to avoid a predator.

 **FACT FILE**

Type of Animal: fish

Length: approximately 4.9 feet (1.5 m)

Habitat: coral and rocky reefs

Distribution: worldwide in warm seas and oceans

Housing Materials: none

Moray Eel

A moray eel lives in a hole or crevice so that it is hidden from predators and prey. Its snakelike body allows it to swim into surprisingly small spaces.

Moray eels hunt mostly at night. A moray eel waits for prey to swim near its hole or crevice. With lightning speed, it grabs the prey. During the day, a moray eel will often stick its head and upper body out of the hole or crevice.

Octopus

An octopus lives in a hole or crevice because its main defense is to hide from predators. Its soft, boneless body allows it to squeeze into very narrow places.

Octopuses feed on fish and crabs at night. An octopus often stays in its hole or crevice and unrolls an arm to catch a passing fish, but it also comes out of its home to hunt for prey. An octopus stays in its hole or crevice during the day.

FACT FILE

Type of Animal: invertebrate

Length: 7.9–24.6 feet (2.4–7.5 m)

Habitat: ocean floor

Distribution: almost worldwide in seas and oceans

Housing Materials: none

Did You Know?

Some types of octopuses leave piles of shells in front of their homes. The piles show what the octopuses have been eating.

A large octopus can hide in a very narrow crevice.

FACT FILE

Type of Animal: invertebrate

Length: 0.5 inch (12 mm)

Habitat: near flowers

Distribution: almost worldwide

Housing Materials: beeswax

European Honey Bee

European honey bees live in colonies in hives made of honeycombs. Hives are used for sheltering, raising young, and storing honey and **pollen** to eat.

Young female worker bees make honeycombs inside a cave, hollow tree, or rock cavity. Honeycombs are sheets of six-sided **cells** made of beeswax. The beeswax is produced by **glands** in the **abdomens** of the young female worker bees.

Did You Know?

European honey bees live in colonies of tens of thousands of bees.

Wild European honey bee hives are often found in hollow trees.

A paper nest made up of small cells is attached to a tree branch.

Did You Know?

Paper wasps live in colonies of up to 500 wasps. They sting people or animals that approach or disturb their nests.

Paper Wasp

Paper wasps live in colonies in paper nests. Paper nests are light but strong homes for the wasps and their young.

A queen paper wasp chews wood and mixes the **fibers** with **saliva** to form a paste. She uses the paste to build a cone-shaped nest with six-sided cells. The queen lays one egg in each cell. She raises the first batch of young, then the first batch raises the second batch.

FACT FILE

Type of Animal: invertebrate

Length: approximately 0.6 inch (16 mm)

Habitat: trees and buildings

Distribution: every continent except Antarctica

Housing Materials: wood fibers and saliva

Mounds and Pots

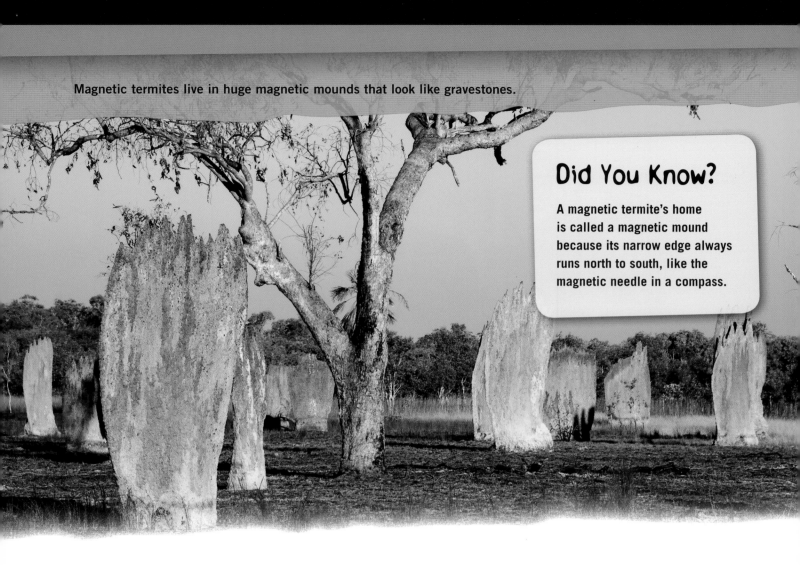

Magnetic termites live in huge magnetic mounds that look like gravestones.

Did You Know?

A magnetic termite's home is called a magnetic mound because its narrow edge always runs north to south, like the magnetic needle in a compass.

FACT FILE

Type of Animal: invertebrate

Length: approximately 0.2 inch (5 mm)

Habitat: grasslands

Distribution: Australia

Housing Materials: soil and saliva

Magnetic Termite

Magnetic termites live in colonies in magnetic mounds. These types of mounds stay at the right temperature and also protect the termites from floods.

The mounds are usually 9.8 to 13.1 feet (3–4 m) high and 9.8 feet (3 m) wide. The wide eastern side of a magnetic mound warms up in the morning sun. Only the thin top edge catches the fierce midday sun. The wide western side catches the afternoon sun.

Potter Wasp

A female potter wasp makes one or more pot-shaped nests out of mud. Her young live in these pots.

Female potter wasps mix mud with saliva and work it into a rounded pot. The saliva stops the mud from crumbling once it dries. When a pot is finished, the female potter wasp lays an egg in it. She puts a caterpillar in the pot for the young to eat and then seals the opening.

FACT FILE

Type of Animal: invertebrate

Length: 0.1–1.2 inches (2–30 mm)

Habitat: near streams and buildings

Distribution: every continent except Antarctica

Housing Materials: mud and saliva

Did You Know?

A potter wasp larva hatches from an egg. The larva becomes a pupa, and an adult then comes out of the pupa. The adult wasp then breaks through the side of the pot.

A female potter wasp attaches her pot-shaped nest to a twig or other object.

FACT FILE

Type of Animal: invertebrate

Length: 0.2–1.6 inches
(5–40 mm)

Habitat: forests, woodlands,
and mangrove swamps

Distribution: Africa, Asia,
Australia, and North and
South America

Housing Materials: silk

Golden Orb-weaving Spider

A golden orb-weaving spider lives in a web. It weaves a golden web out of silk, and the web catches prey for the spider to eat.

A female golden orb-weaving spider releases a silk thread from her **spinnerets** to start a web. The thread is blown by the wind until it becomes attached to a tree. She releases and attaches silk threads until the web is finished. The web is usually about 3.3 feet (1 m) wide.

Did You Know?

A golden orb-weaving spider's web is so strong that it can catch small birds and bats!

A female golden orb-weaving spider usually sits head down in the center of her round web.

A silkworm spins a cocoon around itself when it is ready to turn into a silkworm moth.

Did You Know?

A silkworm cocoon is made of a single thread of silk that is 985 to 2,950 feet (300–900 m) long!

Silkworm

A silkworm spins a cocoon out of silk to use as a temporary home while it is changing into an adult.

Silkworm moths lay eggs on mulberry leaves. A silkworm hatches from each egg and eats mulberry leaves day and night. As it grows, it sheds its skin four times, then it spins a cocoon around itself and changes into a pupa. An adult comes out of the pupa.

 FACT FILE

Type of Animal: invertebrate

Length: 3 inches (75 mm)

Habitat: mulberry trees

Distribution: Asia

Housing Materials: silk

Limpets usually have raised lines, called ribs, on their shells.

Did You Know?

Some types of limpets return to the same place on a rock, known as a "home scar," each time the tide goes out.

Limpet

A limpet's home is its flattened, oval-shaped shell. The shell protects the limpet from the sun, predators, and waves.

Limpets cling tightly to rocks when the tide goes out. A limpet's shell protects it from drying out in the Sun and from predators such as seabirds. Its shell also protects it from pounding waves when the tide comes in. When it is covered in water, a limpet grazes on water plants called algae.

FACT FILE

Type of Animal: invertebrate

Width: 0.4–7.9 inches (1–20 cm)

Habitat: rocky shores

Distribution: worldwide

Housing Materials: none

Hermit Crab

A hermit crab lives in an empty shell to protect its long, soft body from predators. It drags the shell along when it walks around.

As it grows, a hermit crab needs to move into a larger shell. It searches the ocean floor for a shell of the right size. It will hold up and turn over different shells before making its choice.

FACT FILE

Type of Animal: invertebrate

Length: less than 1 inch to 11.8 inches (30 cm)

Habitat: seas and oceans, rocky shores, mangrove swamps, and land

Distribution: worldwide

Housing Materials: none

Did You Know?

Hermit crabs sometimes fight over empty shells. Also, one crab sometimes forces another to give up its shell.

A stolen shell provides a good home for a hermit crab.

FACT FILE

Type of Animal: invertebrate

Width: 1–1.6 inches (2.5–4 cm)

Habitat: seas and oceans

Distribution: worldwide

Housing Materials: none

Whale Barnacle

A whale barnacle has a huge mobile home—a whale! It lives on a whale to get a free ride through food-rich water.

A young whale barnacle will attach itself to a whale and stay on that whale for its whole life. It gathers **plankton** to eat from the water flowing over the whale's skin.

Did You Know?

Although large colonies of whale barnacles are very heavy, the barnacles do not harm the whales on which they live.

Whale barnacles live and grow on different types of whales, such as humpback whales.

A porcelain anemone crab can live in several different types of sea anemones.

Did You Know?

A porcelain anemone crab uses its large claws to fight any anemonefish that try to steal its home—however, the anemonefish usually win the battle.

Porcelain Anemone Crab

A porcelain anemone crab lives in a large sea anemone. The dangerous sea anemone protects the crab from predators.

Porcelain anemone crabs hide among the stinging tentacles of sea anemones. Predators do not try to eat the crabs because they are afraid of being stung by the sea anemones. The crabs do not get stung because they are protected by **mucus**.

 FACT FILE

Type of Animal: invertebrate

Body Width: approximately 1 inch (2.5 cm)

Habitat: seas and oceans

Distribution: worldwide except the Arctic and Antarctic

Housing Materials: none

Lodges and Dams

After building a dam, American beavers build their lodge either on an island or on the banks of the lake that is created.

lodge

Did You Know?

The largest American beaver dam ever found was 2,133 feet (650 m) long!

⬛ FACT FILE

Type of Animal: mammal

Head and Body Length: approximately 2.3 feet (70 cm)

Habitat: streams and rivers

Distribution: North America

Housing Materials: sticks and mud

American Beaver

American beavers live in colonies in homes called lodges. They build lodges with underwater entrances so that predators cannot get in.

Working together, beavers build a wall of sticks and mud, called a dam, across a stream or river. They build a rounded lodge of sticks and mud in the lake that forms upstream of the dam. A lodge protects American beavers from predators, and from snow and ice in the winter.

abdomens	the back parts of insects' or spiders' bodies	**nursing**	feeding with milk
breeding	having young	**plankton**	floating plants and animals
camouflage	to disguise or blend in with the surroundings	**pollen**	the yellow powder in flowers
cells	small compartments	**predators**	animals that hunt and kill other animals for food
colonies	groups of animals of the same type that live close together	**pregnant**	having a baby growing inside
currents	the steady flow of water in a certain direction	**prey**	animals that are hunted and caught for food by other animals
fibers	fine, thread-like pieces	**reptile**	a creeping or crawling animal that is covered with scales
glands	groups of cells in the body that make and release substances	**saliva**	a liquid in the mouth that mixes with food
invertebrate	an animal without a backbone	**spinnerets**	organs in a spider's body that make silk
mammals	animals that feed their young with their own milk	**temporary**	lasting for a short time
marshlands	areas of low, wet land	**vertical**	in an upright position or direction
mucus	a thick, slimy liquid		